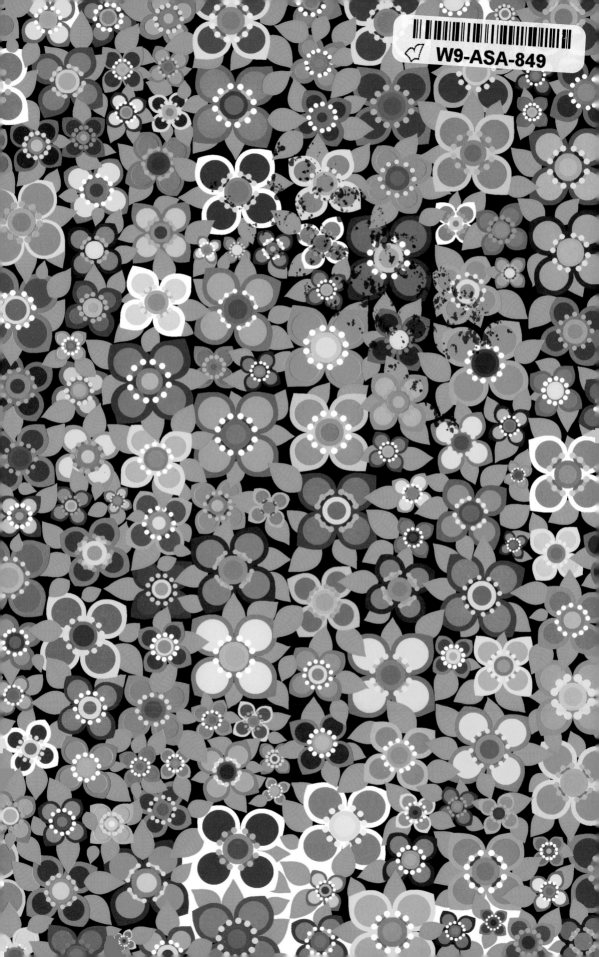
W9-ASA-849

I Will See You Again

LISA BOIVIN

HIGHWATER
PRESS

For my brother Durk

How did it get so dark?
How did you get so dark?
How did you get so far away?
I will fly over an ocean.
I will wrap you in cedar.
I will carry you back into day.

Dear Big Brother,

Our farewell journey began with a phone call from our mom. She told me that you had died. As Mom and I cried together, I decided I would travel to England to bring you home.

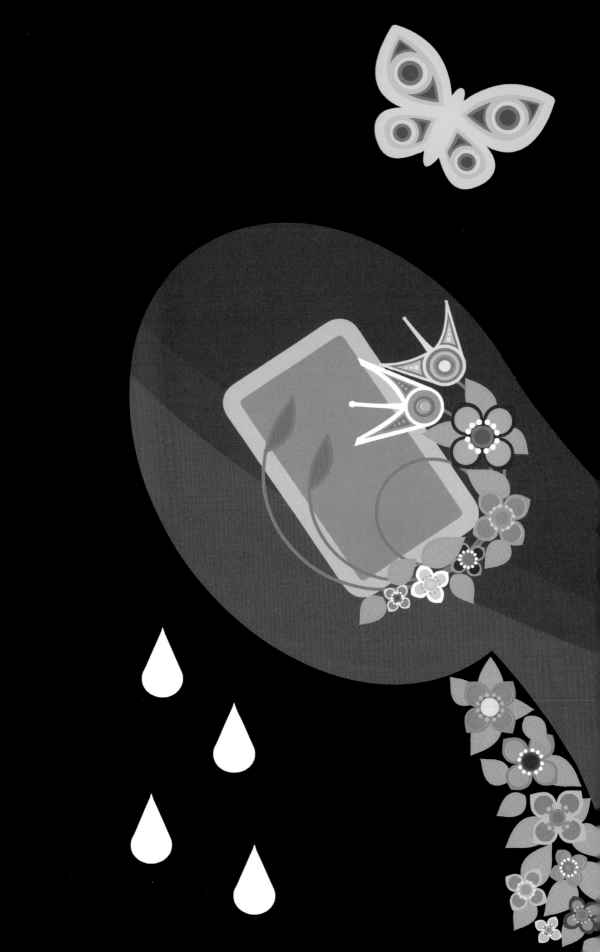

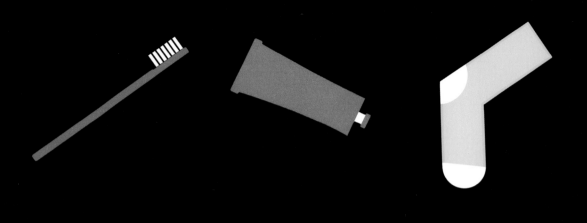

By then, you had been working and living in England for 11 years. I packed my bag quickly so I could travel to England and bring you home to Mom.

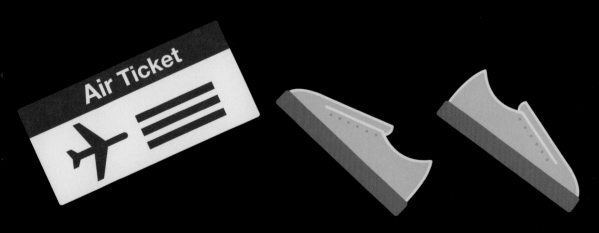

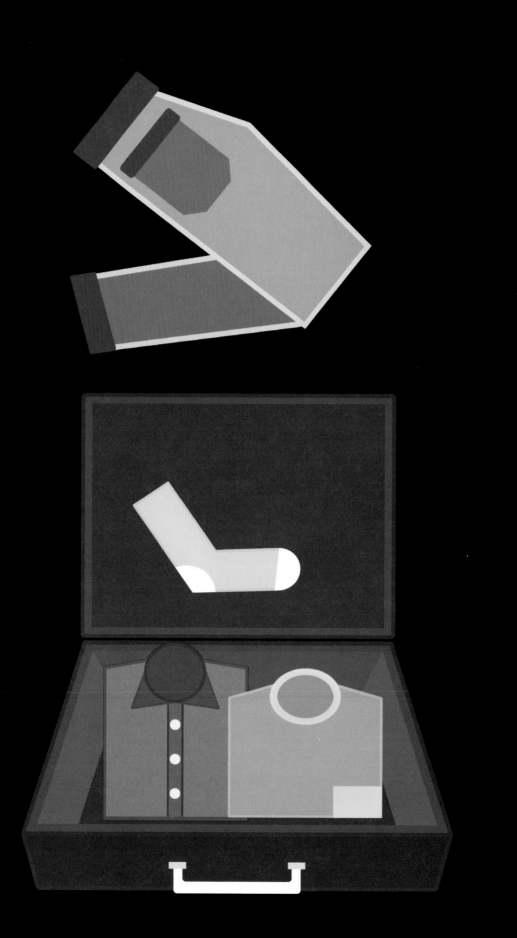

Everything happened so quickly. There was no time to process what was going on. The airport was crowded. The seats on the airplane felt very small. I could not move, and I could not stop thinking about you.

As the plane landed, my tears started to flow. I understood that as soon as I arrived in England, your death would be real. Our family would never be the same because you would be gone.

I picked up your body from the funeral home. You had

chosen to be cremated, which turned your body to ashes.

It felt so strange to hold your body in a small, heavy

box. A box that was once a man. A box that was once my

brother. A few minutes later, the strangeness was gone,

and I felt you near me.

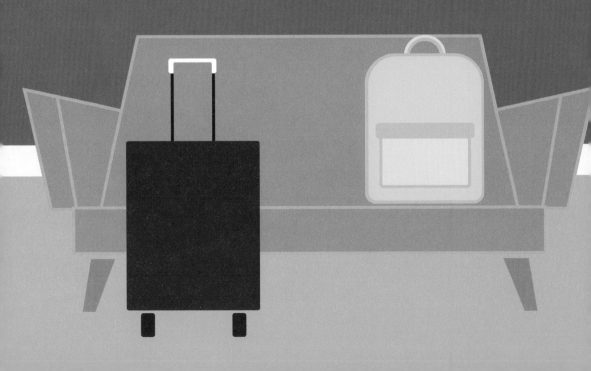

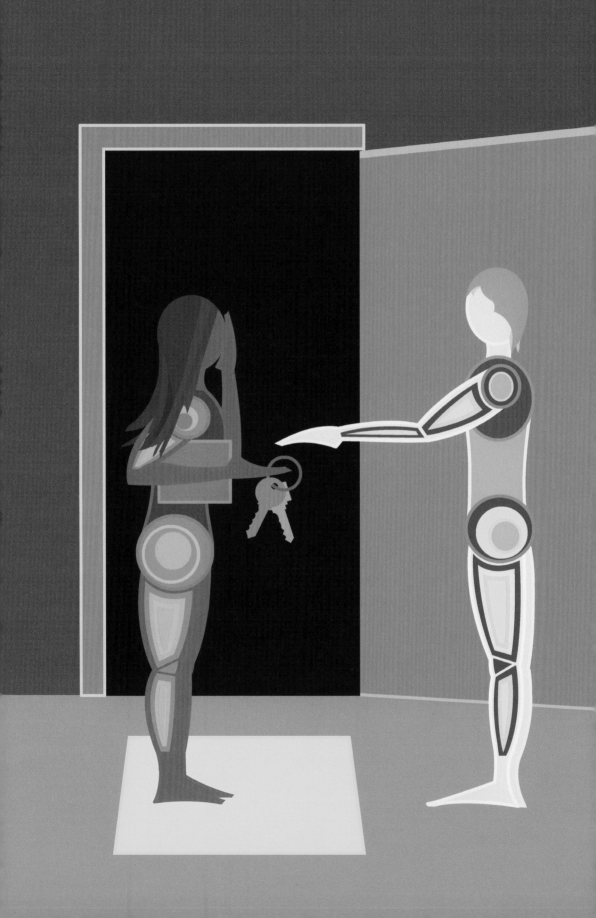

I met your landlord so he could let me into your home.
He told me many things that were hard to hear. You had
not worked for years because you were sick. Your wife
had left, and sometimes you were so sad you would get
confused. Worst of all, you did not have anyone with
you at the end.

There were many documents that needed to be sorted. I opened medical reports and letters informing you of missed appointments. I felt angry that you didn't tell me that you were sick. I was also mad at myself for not asking you if you were okay. Last year I promised to visit but canceled at the last minute. I thought that we would have more time.

Dear Patient,

This letter is to inform you that you missed your last medical appointment.

Dear Doctor,

I am very sorry I missed my appointment. Sometimes I forget things. I live alone and there is no one to remind me of my appointments or to help me with scheduling.

Things to remember

1) Take medication
2) Make doctor's appointment
3) Mail cheque

Going through your photos made me feel better. They reminded me that you were once very much alive. Your photos helped me understand who you were. You were sick for a long time, but you also lived an adventurous life. You traveled to many places and had many careers. You were a teacher, an editor, and a store clerk.

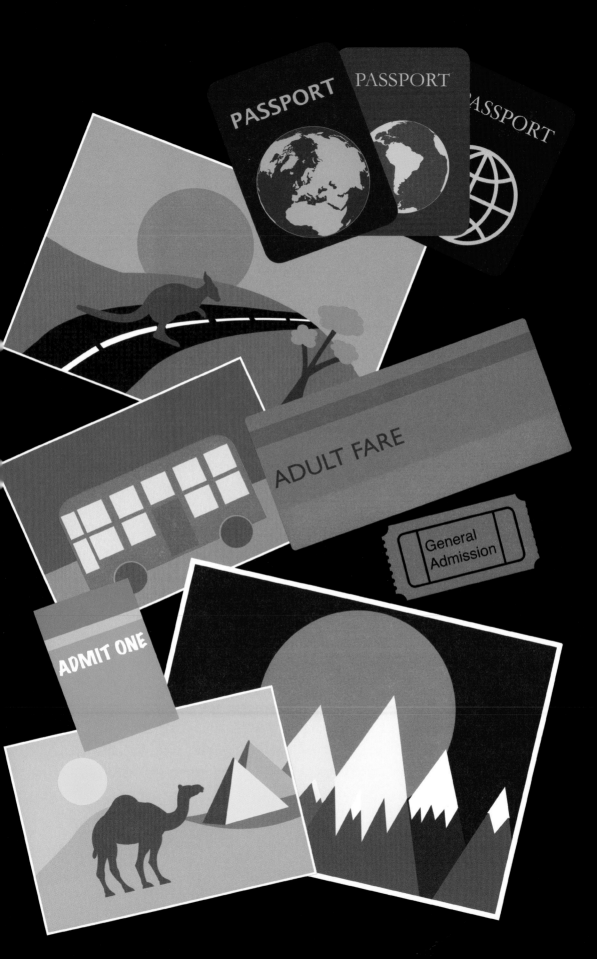

I was tired from my long journey. I fell asleep in your bed.

Your spirit was so powerful, I could feel you spinning

above me. I dreamt of our childhood, and then I traveled

with you to places I had not seen. The dream made me

feel anxious. I knew that you would not hurt me, but I

still had a long journey ahead of me. I had to help you

rest so I could rest.

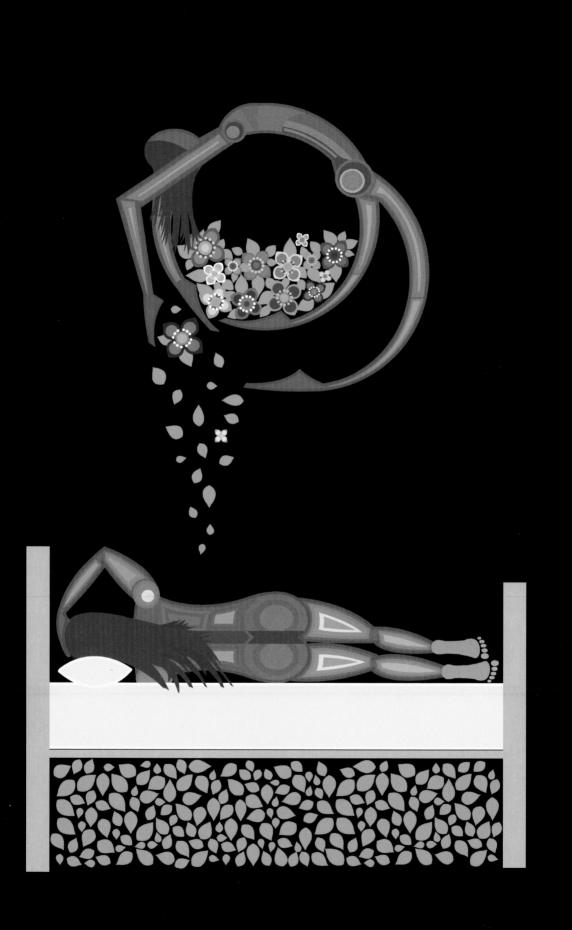

I remembered that cedar helps us to rest. I wasn't sure if cedar grew in England. I went for a walk in the forest to see if I could find some. The forest was so beautiful. I was close to your home. I knew that you had walked where I was walking. I jumped for joy. I felt happy that you had lived in such a beautiful place.

I walked for a long time. I found a cedar tree as the sun was setting.
As I cut cedar branches off, I told the tree why I needed her and
she moved towards me. I knew she understood. I thanked her for
her generosity and then hurried back to your home.

I wrapped you gently with the branches.

Cedar soothed you, and you began to rest.

I had one day free before we would travel home. I wanted to understand how you lived. I went to many different places on your block. I touched every doorknob of the shops that you mentioned in your letters. And I told all the shopkeepers that I was your sister. The owner of the deli told me your favorite order was a BLT sandwich with one sausage on the side. I said, "I will have the same."

When I returned to your home, I could feel that you were lonely. I wanted to do something special for us— something that a sister and brother would do together. I put you in my backpack and went for a walk.

I found a carousel during our walk. I knew that this was

the right thing for us to share.

As the carousel whirled around,

I could feel your spirit laughing.

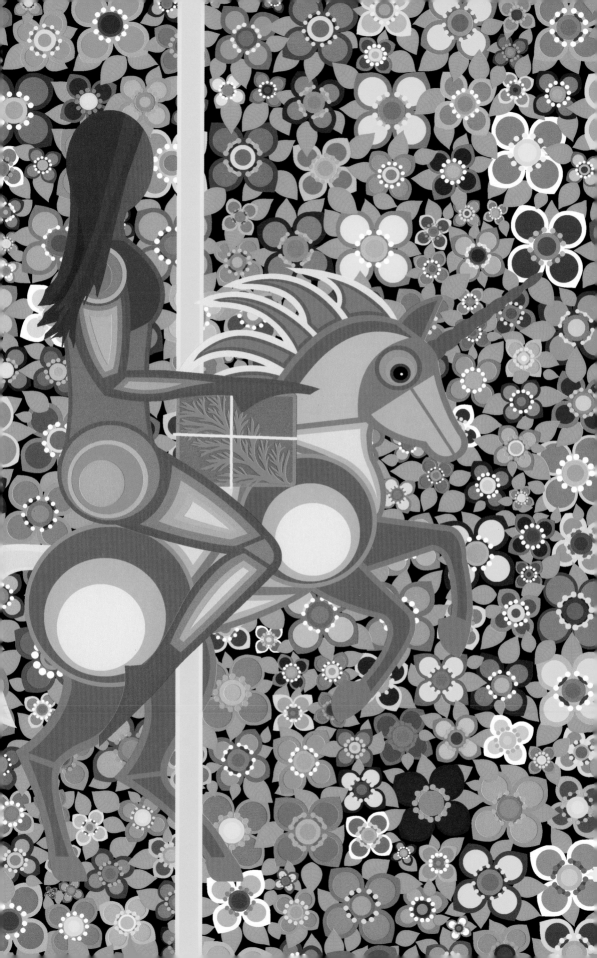

I returned to your home to pack. I wanted to pick the right things for Mom—things of yours that would comfort her. I packed your egg cup, because she would make us soft-boiled eggs when we were kids. I packed your pillowcase. When she was tired, she could put her head down for a nap and dream with you. You let me know it was time to go when you opened your door with a gentle breeze.

As the plane took off, it began to rain. England was crying tears that were both sad and happy. England was sad that you were leaving but happy that you would soon be home with our mom.

Our journey was coming to an end. And just like England, I cried tears that were both sad and happy. I was sad to let you go, but happy because you would soon be safe with Mom. We are always safe with Mom.

Mom was very happy to see us when we arrived. She held her arms open for me to give her a big hug. I could feel you were relieved when I handed you to her.

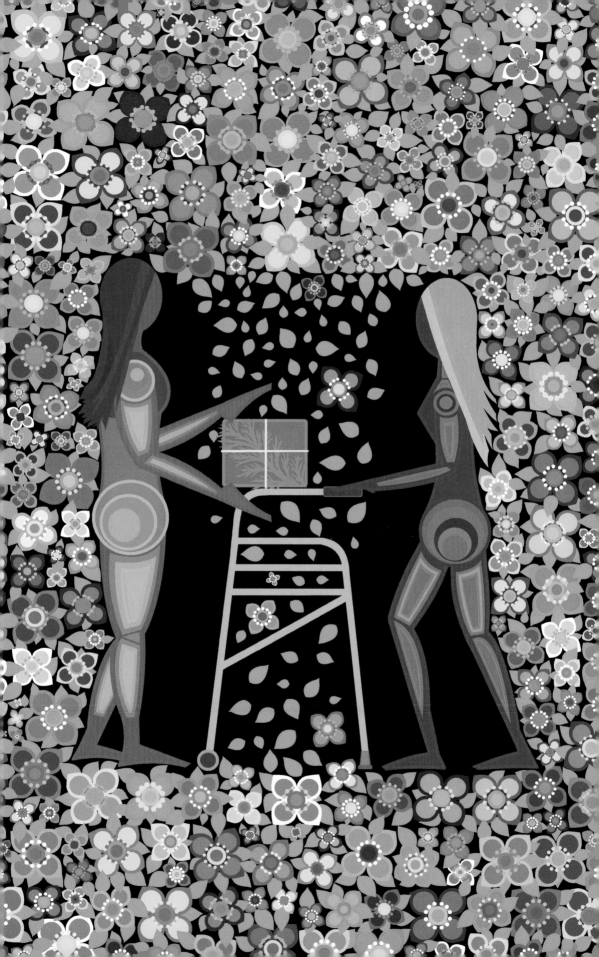

Now that you were home, I think about how we are from
a large family. You are the oldest, and I am the youngest.
I looked at the photos on Mom's wall and realized that, for a
while, it was just you and Mom. Bringing you home to Mom
made me feel happy for you. You are exactly where you are
meant to be. You have left us, but you are also here now.

Mom and I removed the cedar from you, and you began to rest. Just before you fell asleep, I whispered, "I will see you again."

Love always,
Little Sister

© 2020 Lisa Boivin

Excerpts from this publication may be reproduced under licence
from Access Copyright, or with the express written permission
of HighWater Press, or as permitted by law.

All rights are otherwise reserved, and no part of this publication
may be reproduced, stored in a retrieval system, or transmitted
in any form or by any means—electronic, mechanical,
photocopying, scanning, recording or otherwise—except
as specifically authorized.

We acknowledge the support of the Canada Council for the Arts.
Nous remercions le Conseil des arts du Canada de son soutien.

HighWater Press gratefully acknowledges the financial support
of the Province of Manitoba through the Department of Sport,
Culture and Heritage and the Manitoba Book Publishing Tax
Credit, and the Government of Canada through the Canada Book
Fund (CBF), for our publishing activities.

HighWater Press is an imprint of Portage & Main Press.
Printed and bound in Canada by Friesens
Design by Relish New Brand Experience

Library and Archives Canada Cataloguing in Publication

Title: I will see you again / [written and illustrated by] Lisa Boivin.
Names: Boivin, Lisa, 1970- author, illustrator.
Identifiers: Canadiana (print) 20190148373 | Canadiana (ebook)
     20190151374 | ISBN 9781553798552 (hardcover) | ISBN
     9781553798576 (PDF) | ISBN 9781553798569 (iPad fixed
     format)
Subjects: LCSH: Boivin, Lisa, 1970-—Family. | LCSH:
     Bereavement. | LCSH: Tinne Indians—Social life and customs.
Classification: LCC E99.T56 B63 2020 | DDC 155.9/3708972—
     dc23

23 22 21 20   1 2 3 4 5

**HIGHWATER
PRESS**

www.highwaterpress.com
Winnipeg, Manitoba
Treaty 1 Territory and homeland of the Métis Nation